# #NOTCONSUMED
## RECLAIMING YOUR LIFE
## FROM THE GRIP OF CIRCUMSTANCES

# Introduction

I remember so clearly the day my husband moved in with his new girlfriend. I remember it not for the particular details of the moment, but for how it threatened to destroy me.

Although shock held my tears captive as his brake lights faded in the distance, inside my heart was exploding from the pressure. I could literally feel the waters rising violently as they suffocated every hope and dream I had ever mustered.

It wasn't until the door was closed that my legs were no longer able to hold me, and my face planted on the carpet in hysteria. I know I don't need to re-live the rest of the scene for you to understand pain, heartache, and fiery trials. Maybe for you it was a miscarriage, a cancer diagnosis, the death of a loved one, or a lost job that brought you to your knees.

The truth is... life is full of trials that threaten to consume us. When we think of the possible perpetrators we always think of these huge life-altering events. But most of these "big" things are rarely the culprits. Sure there are people who never get back up when life knocks them down, but most of us hold on for our lives with no choice but to trust God.

So what then consumes us? What are the things that hem us in so tightly against the wall that we can't breathe?

Let's consider first the definition of consume. Webster defines it as "to waste or burn away." You see, when we think about a fire consuming a building we rarely consider that it is actually a step-by-step process. The fire starts in one outlet, creeps up a wall, down the carpet and fills the room. Then it creeps into another room. It all happens fast, but rarely does one spark ignite an entire house.

Our lives are consumed in much the same way. It's those not-so-obvious circumstances that creep into one part of our life then another and another until we are "wasted" or "burned out." It's the one insensitive friend on top of the list of too many things to do that causes us to yell at our disobedient child and then drown ourselves in a bucket of ice cream. Which, by the way, makes us feel guilty, fat, and unloved. Can you see where I am going with this?

Little by little we are consuming ourselves and we don't even know it. In fact, we are too busy trying to make it look better (ya know- on social media) and pretending that our lives look like everyone else's to even notice the truth about it all.

But our negligence doesn't change the facts. We are consumed. Burned out. Stressed out. Overweight (well maybe just me). Unhealthy. And most of all unhappy.

Day after day we get back on the hamster wheel chasing some "perfect life" that we are certain has to be out there. We keep pushing forward, doing more and more, and feeling disappointed that we can't seem to get there.

But all of that is about to change. If you are willing to let it, that is. You see, there is a secret to not letting life consume you. There is a way to do it all and have it all. The trouble is, we are just a little confused about the definition of "all." We need to do a little re-defining and a little truth-claiming if we are going to fix this. So what do you say?

Are you in? Are you ready to become #NOTCONSUMED?

♡ Kim

# WHAT ARE YOU CONSUMED WITH?

 So you bought this book. Good. That's half the battle. Just knowing that your life is being held captive by your circumstances is the first step toward taking it back. But the second step is going to involve some work.

If you've never been much of the journaling type, will you consider it just this once? I think you'll get much more out of our time together if you do. You can run down to the Christian bookstore and get something beautiful or just grab an old spiral bound out of the closet. They both work just as well. The key is to find something that you'll use!

For today, just grab a scrap sheet of paper if you don't have a notebook yet. You can transfer your notes later. Don't let the journal thing keep you from completing this crucial task! Whatever it takes, let's do this. Ok?

We need to get to the bottom of what is causing us to be consumed. This probably won't happen today and it's probably a lot deeper than you think. But we have to start somewhere.

## Getting Deeper with God

Open your Bible and read Psalm 139:23-24. Pray and ask God to search your heart and to help you identify the issues that are keeping you from living a victorious life. Make a list of those things in your journal. You'll want to leave lots of space so you can come back and add things as you think of them.

Questions to ask yourself:

> *What makes me nervous or anxious?*
> *What am I worried about?*
> *What am I afraid of?*
> *Is there something that could happen that makes me worried?*
> *What hurts me?*
> *What causes me to feel disappointed?*
> *Why am I frustrated?*
> *Why am I angry?*
> *What causes me to doubt or question God?*

No one will read this but you, so be honest with yourself. The more you write down, the easier it will be to work on fixing those things.

Before you end today, say a prayer and thank God that He is helping you work through this. Don't close the journal with all those negative thoughts in your head. Start now, thanking Him for helping you make these changes!

I'll see you tomorrow.

For extra accountability, consider telling a friend about your list and asking them to pray for you. Sometimes simply admitting that we are consumed with something is the most freeing step in the process.

# GOD'S MERCIES ARE NEW THIS VERY MORNING

 I hope you are not still thinking about that list you made yesterday, but I know better. There is something about making a list of all the things that are consuming us that just has a way of making us feel like a failure.

This is one of my greatest struggles, too. I used to tell myself things like, "You're not a failure" or "You are a good person." Ya know, the things people try and convince us of.

But the truth is, I was failing and I knew it. Telling myself that I wasn't failing didn't help me because it was a big lie. And it's a big lie for you, too. Every single day of our lives we fail at something. It's just the nature of living in a fallen world with sinful flesh.

Good Christians still sin and people who try hard still fail.

*BUT- we are not hopeless.* That, my friend, is the thing we need to be telling ourselves. As we go through this devotional, I want you to keep telling yourself that God's mercies are new every morning. Skip the lies about not being a failure because you are going to mess up again. Focus instead on the hope, grace, and mercy that we have in God, even when we fail over and over again.

## Getting Deeper with God

Read Lamentations 3:19-26 today. As you read, record in your journal WHY and HOW we are not consumed. This verse gives us lots of very specific answers to those questions.

Next, write out Lamentations 3:22-23 on a notecard so you can carry it with you and memorize it. Consider doing this using the KJV if you'd like to keep the phrasing of "not consumed."

I love to sing hymns as a part of my time with God, so I'm going to suggest some that go along with our journey here. It's up to you whether or not you want to use them. You can sing them, write the lyrics out, read the lyrics, and journal about what you learn, etc.

See you tomorrow. I'm praying for you!

Today, sing the hymn "Great is Thy Faithfulness." It was written directly from Lamentations 3:22-23.

## ADMITTING YOU'RE BROKEN

We can't go any further until we clear the air about something. Brokenness. I was once in a Facebook group with other single moms and someone suggested that we were broken. The ladies in the group literally threw fits. Some even left the group they got so upset. It really got me thinking about this whole idea of brokenness. Of course, no one wants to be broken.

But think of it in terms of horses. Of what use to the rancher is a horse that isn't broken?

The truth is, we are all broken. All. It started in the garden and it won't end until Jesus comes back. Even the most "righteous" of us is in deep need of God's healing... but don't take my word for it. Let's dig into God's Word.

## Getting Deeper with God

Read Luke 7:36-50. Pay particular attention to who is broken in this story. Record your thoughts in your journal as you read.

Usually when we read the story we think of the great brokenness of the woman who wept at the feet of Jesus. But I don't think that was the only point Jesus was trying to make here. The woman walked away with her sins forgiven. But the Pharisee- what happened to him? Nothing.

You see, he was too proud to even notice his incredible brokenness. He was too "righteous" to properly greet Jesus and as a result completely missed the blessing of the forgiveness and salvation that the woman received.

So which one are you? Are you the woman (broken and you know it) or the Pharisee (broken and you don't know it)? What I don't want you to miss here is that the Pharisee missed the opportunity for forgiveness and salvation because he failed to see his own need.

I don't want this for you.

If you walk away from this book failing to see the need to make changes in your life, you'll miss the blessing. Not my blessing of course, but the blessing that God has for you.

> The less you see your own brokenness
> the more broken you are.
> ~Dr. John Monroe

I once heard that a broken Christian is much like a broken vase. No matter what you do, it never goes back together in the same way. But that is the exact intent. It's those little broken places that seep out the beautiful work God has done in our lives. Isn't that an amazing picture?

Take a few minutes before you end today and journal a prayer to God about your brokenness. Consider where you are and what you need so we can move forward, growing and changing in HIM! See you tomorrow.

Sing the hymn "Softly and Tenderly" today. This song is such a humble reminder of the incredible grace of our Savior. Even in our brokenness, He's waiting and watching for us to come to Him.

# FIRST THINGS FIRST

Do you mind if I ask you a personal question? When you got up this morning, what was the very first thing you did? How about the 2nd, 3rd, and 4th things?

Now guard your toes... where did God fit into the order?

Before you get defensive, please let me explain why I'm asking. You see, there is a huge belief among Christians that God doesn't really care when you spend time with Him as long as you do it. There is this notion that as long as you fall into bed at night and utter a "thank you, Lord" then you are ok.

I used to be one of those people. I actually said things like, "God wants us to talk to Him all day so I don't have to feel guilty about not having a quiet time this morning." But you and I both know the reality of that. Sure I thanked Him for the good little things when they came up, but overall we truly didn't have a good relationship.

I'm certain this had a lot to do with the many times in my life when I let circumstances completely consume me. But I eventually learned a hard lesson that I'd like to share with you.

So, first let me apologize for stepping on your toes, but in all love, would you bear with me while I show you why I HAD to make changes and why you might be compelled to as well?

## Getting Deeper with God

Read Psalm 90:14-17. Make observations about this passage in your journal.

Unless you are reading KJV (which says "early") you will notice a very specific time of the day mentioned in verse 14. Did you catch it? Now I'm not suggesting this verse implies that if we don't spend time with God in the morning we are sinful heathens. I'm not willing to get that legalistic about it.

But what I do notice is that the Psalmist is asking God to satisfy him in the morning SO THAT he may rejoice in his circumstances. Pretty cool, huh? Makes me think of the saying "first things first." If we can start our day with the right perspective, it changes the course of the day, doesn't it? The Bible promises that starting our day with God even changes the way we see our circumstances.

I think this is a pretty strong case for spending some time with God before you do anything else. Don't you want to have that joy over your circumstances?

Now before you start with the excuses, I promise I know them all. I know the life where babies cry all night or someone throws up for hours. I know what it is like to have no help at all and to feel like you can't do it for one more minute. I know crazy work schedules and many other difficult situations. They are real... and they rob us of our time with God.

But the truth is, we make this spending time with God thing harder than it needs to be. I don't think we are required to sit down and have an hour-long Bible study with hymns, praying, and deep theological learning first thing every morning. (I do think all of those things should be done on a regular basis, but they don't need to be early.) What needs to be early is just our satisfaction with God.

I can't tell you what this looks like for you, but I think it's a lot more about our heart and our thoughts than it is about what we do in that specific moment. If you need to save deep Bible reading for later, why not read a Psalm to start your day?. Maybe journal a prayer or sing a hymn. I most enjoy just sitting quietly and listening. You could even read a quick devotional like this one. Just do something to spend time with God and in His Word.

Before you close today, take a minute to jot down some sort of commitment in your journal regarding your time with God in the mornings. What do you want to change or do? Write it out and aim to do it!

But whatever you do, don't allow yourself to feel defeated or frustrated over this. Just try, and keep trying. Each day is a new opportunity to start with God. He's not making a list of all the times we fail. He just blesses the times we do spend with Him.

Want an example of how I structure my time with God? Check it out here. bit.ly/1JMWdL4

# IT'S TIME YOU KNOW THE TRUTH

I hope your toes are feeling a little better after our talk yesterday. I also hope you know that I only did it because I love you. In fact, that's the reason for this entire book. I got so tired of watching friends, family, and peers let life's circumstances consume them. I wanted to get on the rooftop and shout, "There's a better way!" But since I don't have a ladder, I opted for this instead. (Ha ha.)

Seriously, I'm so thrilled that you are still reading this devotional. Good for you!

Over the next few weeks I'm going to share with you many strategies that helped me not only survive the fire, but walk through it without even being singed. I pray that God will speak to you and show you areas where you need to grow and change.

If you are going to grow, there is one very important thing you will need as your foundation: truth. You will want to know for sure that you are basing your life's principles, thoughts, and actions on truth.

There's really only one way to do that: read God's Word. I know you know this already. But there is a difference between what we know and what we practice. So I have to ask, are you practicing? Are you filling yourself with God's Word on a daily (or almost daily) basis?

# Getting Deeper with God

Let's do a little Bible exploring today. Read the following verses and record any truths that you find about God, yourself, or your situation.

Isaiah 54:5
Exodus 15:26
Isaiah 9:6
Psalm 68:20
Revelation 17:14
1 John 4:4
Psalm 56:8-11
Jeremiah 29:11
Ephesians 1 (whole chapter)
John 16:33
Jeremiah 31:3

I know that's a lot. No need to dig deep. We are going to talk about some of these as we go along. For now, just bask in the truth of who God is and start thinking about how you can fit more Bible reading time into your day. Make a written commitment in your journal if you are ready.

I'll see you tomorrow!

How are you doing with memorizing Lamentations 3:22-23? Get your card out today and practice.

# WHY ARE YOU MEDITATING ON LIES?

 Someone handed me a Coke and I sat down in the chair, shook the can, and popped the top open. Little bubbles started to fizz up and within a nanosecond, that little old Coke can became a geyser of sticky awfulness that I'm certain rivaled Old Faithful. (At least in my 5th grade mind anyway.)

It was in my hair. All over my clothes. Even down in my shoes. I had to actually leave the birthday party it was so bad.

Looking back, it makes me chuckle. Not so much at the humiliation I felt, but at my naivete. You see, I thought you had to shake it.

I personally caused the geyser of sticky that ultimately humiliated me until I was nearly 20. (Ok, maybe not that long, but it's safe to say that I am still extra cautious with cans of soda.)

This little soda situation reminds me of something we need to be very careful of.

Like that Coke can, our lives are constantly under intense pressure. We battle the enemy, our flesh, circumstances, world influences. The list goes on and on.

On occasion, someone or something shakes that pressure up even more and we've got the perfect storm. We "open the can" and "vent" all over the place, spewing ugly on anything in our path.

As a person who spends the better part of her day interacting on the internet, I see people "vent" like this on a daily basis. Someone will pop into a private group or even post on their personal timeline something that starts with, "I need to vent" or "Warning: this is a rant." Of course, we are pretty guilty of doing this in real life, too. Whether it's in front of a friend, spouse, child, or even just ourselves, this venting thing is killing us.

We've been fed the lie that venting our emotions will make us feel better. But venting actually works against us. Remember the sticky Coke that spewed all over me? Venting our emotions spews the same kind of awful and we don't realize it. All those ugly words ooze in our hair, our clothes, and even down in our shoes. And they stick with us.

But as a Christian, we have a two-fold responsibility for what we say. First, we are accountable for how it affects us and second for how it affects our witness. We can't keep spewing ugly all over ourselves and others.

## Getting Deeper with God

Let's see what God says. Read James 1:26, 2 Corinthians 10:5, and Philippians 4:8. Note in your journal the specific things that God tells us regarding the things we say AND THINK. Also notice the specific things He tells us to think about. Underline them in your Bible.

Thinking and saying negative things about yourself or your circumstances is keeping you consumed. In a real sense, you are meditating on these ugly lies over and over again. This kind of meditation can lead us to believe the lies, change our hearts, doubt our faith, and even turn away from God.

We MUST take hold of this behavior. Stop it as soon as it starts and replace it with truth about God. (Use your list from day 5.)

Practice this today in your journal by replacing a few of those negative thoughts with true things. Write the true things in your journal. Don't skip this. I mean it. ☺

Consider putting a list of truths on the fridge so you can review them often and run to them when you need to replace the lies that keep coming back.

# WRITE THE TRUTH ON YOUR HEART

I've been going to church since I could walk. Growing up it was 3 times a week: Sunday morning, night, and Wednesday night. If the church doors were open, we were there. I remember years of VBS, Girls in Action club, multiple youth camps, lock-ins, and revivals.

But none of that was enough.

When I was 21, my husband of one year left me. The word devastating doesn't do it justice. I was now used, abused, thrown out, alone in a city 24 hours from home, and hopeless.

Despite decades of church attendance and continual hearing of God's truth, I couldn't recall anything that would help me in the moment. Instead of running to God, I ran away. In fact, I went 3 years without stepping foot in a church. My husband was in seminary and I figured that "God's people" were to be avoided at all costs.

I was bitterly and horribly angry at God. Fortunately my story took a turn back in the right direction many years later, but I don't want you to miss the point.

When things got tough, I didn't have what I needed to rely on God. We often fail to rely on God in difficult moments because we can't remember the truth. It gets drowned out by lies, what ifs, and thoughts of what we "deserve."

For the past two days we have talked about knowing and meditating on God's truth. That's a really good start, but if we are going to walk victoriously through the storms of life, we will need a little bit more.

## Getting Deeper with God

Psalm 119:9-16. In your journal, make a list of the steps that you will need to take in order to have a pure life or path.

When it comes to the use of God's Word, we see words like store up, delight, and meditate. The Psalmist gives a clear picture as to why I failed as a young adult to cling to God when life got rough. I had heard the truth over and over again, but I didn't have much memorized (stored in my heart) and Bible reading was something I really only did in church.

Today is the last day I'm going to emphasize this point, but from the bottom of my heart, I beg you to "get it" today. From this moment forward can you commit to read, meditate on, and memorize God's Word? I'm with you on this journey. I promise it's worth it.

I've got a free set of printable Scripture cards for you. I keep them in a 3x5 box and refer to them as various issues resurface in my life. These are also fantastic verses to start memorizing if you aren't sure where to begin. bit.ly/1Q25HUK

# YOU HAVE THIS HOPE

I remember the very day that I knew I was pregnant with my first child. Being a mom was my dream come true. It was the thing I had worked so hard for and that positive pregnancy test was the best present anyone had ever given me.

We left the doctor that day and told everyone we could find. The guy at Wendy's who really just wanted to sell me a soda, the lady at Target who had no idea how premature the baby outfit purchase was, and of course the entire universe on Facebook.

Within two weeks of that day, everything changed. I had a little spotting and rushed in for an ultrasound which revealed no heartbeat. The dream-come-true had turned into a nightmare. We had to wait a week to be sure there was no growth, but the repeat ultrasound revealed the same story.

I won't lie. It was the worst thing I had ever felt in my whole life. There were so many unknowns about my ability to carry a baby, fears that we might not conceive again, and people who would need to be told.

I was such a weak Christian then, but I knew that this had to be God's plan and so I knew I had to accept it.

By the time I went in for the D&C (to remove any lingering tissue) I felt a deep peace over my heart. I was focusing on the blessings that I did have and the hope I had in Christ. I laid there in the hospital bed with a curtain in between us and the next person on my doctor's list. It was easy to hear her sobbing. She occasionally wept aloud to her husband over the loss and my heart broke. For the first time in my life I realized that I had something not everyone had. The two of us were walking through the exact same circumstance, yet my soul was quieted by the hope I had in an almighty God.

## Getting Deeper with God

Read **1 Peter 1:3-7 and Hebrews 6:19-20.** Write the letters HOPE in a large block form in your journal, then record keywords that you read from these two passages. You can use the two verses I list below, too!

I hope you didn't miss the first part of 1 Peter 1:6. Go back and make sure you saw what our response should be to this hope.

I know it doesn't necessarily take the pain or tears away, but just knowing that God keeps His promises can bring so much hope. There will be a day with no more tears (Rev. 21:4), no more pain, and no more fears. He who promised it will do it.

> **"And now, O Lord, for what do I wait?
> My hope is in you." Psalm 39:7**

I am praying this over you today... "May the God of hope fill you with all joy and peace in believing, so that by the power of the Holy Spirit you may abound in hope." Romans 15:13

# TAKE FEAR CAPTIVE

Fear has defined me. In 2000, I slept with every light on for almost an entire year. Then I got over it only to fall back into the same pattern a few years later. I simply don't do ALONE very well. In fact, I'd rather get a root canal than be in a dark and quiet house without a man to protect me.

But I don't have that option. Every night is dark and quiet. Every night. And sometimes, it's more than I can bear. At times, I have allowed fear to regain its hold over me. I've fallen back into sleeping with the lights on, triple-checking locks, and holding my phone on my chest (as if that is somehow going to save me).

While safety is certainly one of my biggest issues, fear has taken other places in my heart captive as well.

Fear that I would not be enough.
Fear that I would not graduate.
Fear that I would be hurt or die.
Fear that he wouldn't love me.
Fear that I would mess up my kids.
Fear that eating something would make me sick.
Fear that the bank would be robbed while I'm inside.
Fear that a car would run the stoplight and hit me.
Fear that I would be homeless.
Fear that right would not win or justice would not prevail.
Fear of that which is unknown.

In fact, I find that sometimes I have been more afraid of what could or might be than what really is. I have let fear control my thoughts and my actions.

After years of hard work, my struggle with fear has been mostly overcome. (Although I sometimes need a reminder.) But how about you? Are you living in fear? Is this a source of recurring struggle for you (like me)?

# Getting Deeper with God

Read Isaiah 41:10-13. Record in your journal what you learn about God and fear. Next, write verse 10 in first person. Here is my example. "I will not fear for God is with me. I will not fear for He is my God. He will strengthen me and help me. He will uphold me with His righteous right hand."

Try the same exercise with these verses: 2 Timothy 1:7, Psalm 27:1, Psalm 112:7.

When fear creeps in, follow these steps:
1. Recognize that the enemy wants you to be afraid so you will not believe God. Refuse to let him have the satisfaction.
2. Declare truth out loud. When fear creeps in, tell it to leave in the name of Jesus. Declare your safety and security out loud. Read or recite Scripture over the enemy and his deceptive thoughts. Keep a list of verses handy at all times. (We have a section for fear in the cards that I gave you on day 7, plus a printable below.)
3. Pray and ask God to help you feel secure. Then praise Him for all He has done. Focusing your thoughts on the greatness of God will keep you from dwelling on your circumstances.
4. Put verses in every corner of the house and read them. Make them personal and declare them out loud. Memorize at least one to fall back on when you need it.
5. I'm praying for you as you battle whatever makes you feel afraid. God will always prevail and His plans are perfect!

You can download a free printable of the verses we discussed today to hang on the fridge or put by your bed. bit.ly/1nRuwfp

## FOR THE UNLOVED...

 Perhaps you've heard of Corrie ten Boom. She was a Dutch Christian who hid Jews from the Nazis during the Holocaust. She and her entire family were taken to a concentration camp during a raid in 1944.

As you can imagine, conditions in the camp were deplorable. Corrie's dad died within 10 days of the raid. Her sister, Betsie, fell ill very quickly because of the flea infested conditions and the lack of adequate rations.

On her deathbed as she was agonizing in pain from the lack of care, Betsie said these words to her sister. (Corrie is credited with them as she penned them in her autobiography.)

> There is no pit so deep that
> God's love is not deeper still.
> ~Corrie ten Boom

Wow. To be beaten, abused, starved, shamed, worked harshly, bitterly cold... and yet utter these words. I would find it hard to be true if I hadn't experienced it myself. When I found myself in the deepest pit of despair, God's love was deeper.

He never left me, just as He promised. There was no place I could go where He couldn't wrap His loving arms around me. And this is true for you, too.

## Getting Deeper with God

Read Psalm 36:5-9. Write (or draw) what comes to mind as you read these verses about God's love. Then continue on with the ones listed below.

Psalm 34:18
Jeremiah 31:3
Romans 8:35-39
Zephaniah 3:17

Try summarizing the love of God in your journal in light of those verses. I don't want to do this much for you as it will mean so much more to you if you do it yourself. But... I am praying that through this exercise you will see how deep and immeasurable God's love is for you. Nothing can separate you from His everlasting love. He chose you, rejoices over you, and will always be there for you. How's that for love?

Consider singing the hymn "I Stand Amazed in the Presence" today. I can't think of a better way to grasp the love of God!

# WHEN YOU FEEL WEAK

Sometimes when life is hard, we can't understand the purpose. There were many people in the Bible who surely felt this way. Like Joseph, who spent the better part of 13 years being punished over and over again for things he really didn't do. Or Abraham, who followed God to Canaan, only to find a famine, and David who spent a few decades hiding in caves even AFTER God anointed him as King.

When things seem so hard, of course we're tempted to shake our fists at heaven and shout, "Why, God?"

Can you imagine the "fist shaking" that Job might have wanted to do? Despite his righteous faith he lost his property, wealth, family, and health. But... his response to God is one of the most humbling in the Bible. "The Lord gave and the Lord has taken away; blessed be the name of the Lord." (Job 1:21 ESV)

I don't know about you, but I would love to have the kind of faith that would offer up that kind of response. But it's not easy. When storms are raging in our homes, it's hard to have faith. It's hard to keep going. I can remember days when it was hard to even get out of bed or open my eyes.

But here's the truth: Faith is like a muscle. It gets stronger with use. Even if we feel weak, this working out of our faith is growing us strong. If you read the Psalms, you see David go through this exercise over and over again. Each time, he clings to the Lord as his rock and salvation.

# Getting Deeper with God

Are you feeling weak and weary today? I love the words of Romans 1:17 as an encouragement for anyone who feels weak. Write them in your journal. If you will, use the KJV version because the wording is a little more clear.

How is God revealed to us? Circle or highlight it in your Bible and journal.

I hope you saw that God is revealed to us through our faith. This trial is actually our personal appointment with God. (How cool is that?) I also love the thought that God carries us from FAITH to FAITH.

No matter what comes in life, all we have to do is keep hanging on to God "from faith to faith." The more we do, the stronger we become and the more God is revealed to us. Finish out today by reading Psalm 121 and enjoy the fact that YOU get a personal appointment with God!

Did you finish memorizing Lamentations 3:22-23? If so, move on and pick another Scripture that is meaningful to you. If not, keep pressing on. You'll get it!

# DON'T JUMP

I know that your circumstances may seem very dark right now. But today I want to talk to you about something that I have been so burdened about. You see when things get tough in their lives, most people have one of two responses: fight or flight. They either resolve to get through this or they try to get away from it.

I have to confess that I've been a runner. In fact, I spent the better part of 5 years running from God. The tunnel got dark and I jumped off the train. I figured that if God loved me, He would never have let these things happen to me. I stopped going to church and wanted nothing more to do with God.

Maybe you've felt this, too. The thick of the darkness makes it so hard to see that we get scared, start doubting God, and find ourselves wanting to jump off the "train."

BUT- I can promise you it doesn't work. Not only did jumping off cause all kinds of pain in my life, it left me feeling even more broken and empty. Swearing off God only left me with no hope at all to help me with the darkness.

> When the train goes through a tunnel and
> it get's dark, you don't throw away
> the ticket and jump off. You sit still
> and trust the engineer.
> ~Corrie ten Boom

Thankfully, a praying grandmother and a loving and gracious God wooed me back to the truth. It was a hard lesson to learn, but one that I am so thankful for as many years later I would be faced with another tunnel. Only this one much darker: abandoned, unloved, evicted from my home, shamed into food stamps, labeled single mom, and the list went on and on.

I knew the results of jumping, so this time I sat still. I trusted the one who was in control of the entire universe (and thus my situation) and I found the kind of peace that most people will never know. Although I can not even fathom her trial and wouldn't dream of comparing, I can grasp the faith that led Corrie ten Boom to say these words. In the darkest, blackest of circumstances who else can you trust?

## Getting Deeper with God

Read Isaiah 50:10-11. What are two things verse 10 lists as instructions for those who walk in darkness? Circle both of the words in your Bible.

I hope you saw that we are called to trust and rely on God. That's a nice thought, but it's important to note that it's not a request. Read verse 11 carefully. This verse is referring to people who "jump off" or make their own way when things get tough. Literally it means "equip yourselves."

Have you ever been guilty of equipping yourself? This is the idea of trying to fix your own problems or help God out. At first it may seem harmless. I mean after all God helps those who help themselves, right?

Wrong. You won't find that lie in the Bible. Instead you find the end of verse 11. Read it again and see the consequence we face for making our own way.

Depending on the translation, you'll find torment or sorrow. Now think about it. Is that really the end result you are looking for? Of course not. As hard as it may seem, we have to fasten ourselves into this train and sit still. Trust your engineer (God). He created you, loves you, and works all things for your good.

Yes, it's dark, but He knows where you are going. And He alone can be trusted. You... just need to sit still.

If you haven't read the autobiography of Corrie ten Boom, consider doing so. Her faith is one of the most inspiring stories of all time.

# VICTORY... HOW DO WE GET IT?

So far in this book we've looked at a few foundational truths. We've learned that we need to be in the Word, replace lies by memorizing truth, and take captive the fear that is trying to keep us focused on our circumstances.

These are the basics for how to walk humbly with the Lord, but what happens when the water begins to rise?

I'll be honest, I felt like I had a pretty good grip on my faith until my husband left. I was very active in church, participated in regular Bible studies, and was constantly seeking ways to be more like Christ. I loved my life.

The announcement of the affair was much like some sort of freak flash flood or unexpected tornado that came by night and left everything unrecognizable. I had no hints of turmoil or discontent in our marriage. I didn't feel the water rising at all and because of that, I nearly drowned.

Don't miss this, my friend. **Whether you are facing a circumstance that has built up over time or one that has snuck in like a tornado, we are all in just as much danger of drowning.** We need to be prepared to weather whatever storm life brings us, even if one is not on the horizon today. So let's dig in.

## Getting Deeper with God

Read Isaiah 43:1-5, 19. Savor the words of this text and the promises that God gives us here. For each verse, jot down something that God promises you.

I've read this passage at least 100 times. Even today as I write this and read through it again, it brings tears to my eyes. Verse 2 promises us that when we pass through the waters of hard times, God will be with us. When we walk through the fiery trials of life, we will not be consumed.

This is the promise that we will cling to as we consider how to go about the practical parts of gaining VICTORY in our circumstances. Be ready tomorrow as we begin to look at each letter in the word VICTORY to help us walk step-by-step through the storms of life.

We've made a beautiful printable version of Isaiah 43. You can print it and hang it somewhere so you'll never forget. Maybe even frame it! Find it here: bit.ly/1mmbqwN

# V IS FOR VISION CHECK

When I was 11 years old, I got glasses.

What I remember most about that day was the first tree I saw when we walked outside. I looked up at this giant object that I had seen countless times in my life and declared, "Mom, did you know that leaves were each individual pieces of the tree?"

All this time I had thought that trees were just some sort of hazy green collection, sorta like you see in impressionistic paintings. I had NO IDEA that each leaf was an individual unit. (Go ahead and laugh, I'm over it. Haha.) When you see trees portrayed in children's books, they are almost always one big clump of leaves. They rarely appear as individual leaves. Plus, I grew up in Florida where the leaves stay on the trees for the most part.

So my conclusion was based on my own reality and that reality was flawed. I hope you aren't laughing so hard that you miss my point. **Often in life, we see things based on our limited knowledge of that thing.**

Your life is like that tree. The circumstances you face are rarely exactly the way you see them. That's because you are missing the glasses that you need to truly understand and see each part of God's plan concerning this. Your human vision is flawed. And your conclusions will be based largely upon assumptions you make and things you see in that moment.

So, if we know that we don't have the ability to look through God's glasses to get our vision with 100% clarity, we need to make a huge effort to check the truth that is backing up our vision so we are not tempted to despair in the evidence of the moment.

## Getting Deeper with God

Read Proverbs 2:10-11. Draw some sort of image in your journal to help you visualize what the verse is saying. Don't get caught up in making it look beautiful. You can just write the words, draw arrows and use stick figures. Trust me, it will be a meaningful way to meditate on this verse.

Can you think of any examples in your life when you didn't see the whole picture and thus your vision was flawed? What happened? Consider how the circumstance may have been viewed differently if you had backed up your "view" with the truth of God's Word instead of what was most evident in the moment.

Praying for you. See you tomorrow!

Check-up time... how are you doing with your Bible reading? Memorization? Have you seen any improvement in your goals? Take a minute and evaluate yourself, renew your commitment, and plan changes if necessary.

# I- INVITE JESUS INTO THE MESS

As you saw yesterday, we must be meditating on the truth of our circumstances if we are going to rise above them. Knowing the truth is going to make all the difference. But the truth alone will not be enough to help us.

Think about the Pharisees. They were some of the most knowledgeable people who walked this earth when Jesus was among them. They had poured their lives into knowing God's laws and Scriptures. They were desperate for a savior, but when He came they completely missed it.

They missed it because they were unwilling to see Him in a way that was different from what they had planned. <=== Go back and read that again. Write it on your forehead.

I know that you are as guilty of this as I am. We find ourselves in difficult or despairing circumstances and we totally miss Jesus because we are so busy looking for Him to do a particular thing.

If we are going to rise above our circumstances and reclaim our lives from the grip of despair, we will have to invite Jesus into this mess. We can't close the door, pretend it's not happening, or simply ride the waves until the storm is over. All of those reactions are dangerous. They lead to a lack of faith and trust, despair, and even bitterness.

So, how do we invite Jesus into our mess?

# Getting Deeper with God

There are many verses that speak to this topic. Let's just read two that demonstrate what the Word says we can do when we need the Lord to intervene in our situation: Matthew 7:7-8 and Jeremiah 33:3. Journal any possible applications that you see.

Have you prayed and invited Jesus to come into your circumstances? Ask Him for the resolution you desire, but don't forget to ask Him to be with you, comfort you, hold your hand, make you strong, and grow you as you walk through this. Tell Him your thoughts and fears just as you would your closest friend.

I'm praying with you!

Sing "Just a Closer Walk With Thee" today, asking God to fill your empty spaces with His amazing grace.

# C- CHOOSE YOUR RESPONSE

If there was one thing in life that I was certain I never EVER wanted, it was a divorce. My marriage was the most sacred thing I had. Although it was far from perfect, there was nothing that I wasn't willing to do to keep it. I loved my husband dearly and knew that my kids needed a strong, godly dad. Not to mention, I was a stay-at-home mom who hadn't worked in 10 years (and had let her teaching license lapse). I had 3 small children and one on the way. Our mortgage was expensive and our lifestyle was far from frugal.

Divorce was absolutely NOT an option for me.

You can imagine how I felt that night as I watched his brake lights fade into the distance. It's somewhat of a haze. I don't remember ever leaving the doorway. Or eating. Or putting the kids to bed. I don't remember when my friend came over or how she even got word of what was happening.

What I remember was lying on the floor in my living room with my face literally planted in the carpet, my legs tucked into my body, and the heat of 1000 fallen tears burning my cheeks. I remember the words that my friend uttered to me as I faced the rubble of what seemed like the storm that had destroyed us all.

She said, "Kim, you have to go through this. You can't change that. You are not in control of this situation. BUT- you are in control of your response to it. Will you grow from it? Or will you die?"

In a moment where it seemed that absolutely NOTHING was in my control, my sweet friend reminded me that I indeed was in control of something. I may not have been in control of the situation, but I had complete control over how I would respond to it.

You see, I had to choose whether or not I would trust God to work in my life or ignore God and spiral into a pit of despair that was filled with bitterness, brokenness, and a lifetime of darkness.

**I got to choose.**

And so do you. No matter what happens to you in life, you can still choose your response to it. Whether it's your fault or theirs, it doesn't matter. No one has the power to choose your response.

And your choice is the difference. It's the thing that will keep you from drowning. All the right knowledge and "God-talk" won't be enough if you choose not to believe it. You get to choose. What will it be?

## Getting Deeper with God

Read Deuteronomy 30:19-20. These words were spoken by Moses as he was preparing to step down as the leader of the Israelites. He had walked with them through countless grumblings, complaining, and disobedient acts. They had spent 40 years wandering in the wilderness simply because they were afraid to do what God told them to do. And so Moses gives them this charge.

Now I must ask you. What is your choice? Lay aside all the circumstances that you cannot change and look at the one thing you can. Journal and write about what specific ways you can choose your response despite the storm around you.
I'm cheering for you!

I made a printable version of each step of the VICTORY process. Click here: bit.ly/1otQuG7

# T IS FOR TRUST

 The day was ordinary. Down the hall, I could hear the buzz of children happily playing and the hum of the washing machine busily making things clean. There was no reason to expect any hint of turmoil until I stepped in it.

Purple goo oozed between my toes and onto my pant legs. A million scenarios flashed before my mind. Then I saw it. The laundry soap container had plummeted into a dismal sea of purple.

The bottle itself had just come home from the store. And now I found myself mopping up what seemed like gallons of soap. Tears invaded and hysteria settled in my heart. There was no way to salvage the disaster and the $14 to buy a new one would be costly, to say the least. My tired hands pressed and mopped at the goo which easily made its way into the deepest crevices of the carpet. After what seemed like hours of useless pressing, I gave up. The pressures of the day mounted and I fell into a heap of despair.

What was left was a not-even-full cup of laundry soap and a rather damaged vessel. It all seemed so silly. It was just laundry soap. It really shouldn't have been such a big deal. But sometimes my lot hardly seemed fair, and that particular day was the perfect example.

But God had in mind to show me just how powerful He really is. Months passed with the broken vessel of purple doom sitting on my laundry shelf. Days would pass and laundry would pile up. I would empty the tiny cup into the machine with each new load of laundry. And somehow, every time I came back, the cup had just enough left again.

At first, I didn't think much of it, but eventually I found myself wondering. *Didn't I empty it all? How is this cup full again?* But despite my questioning, it was full again. Load after load would wash clean. Fall became winter. Winter began to bloom and still the cup did not grow empty. At first it seemed a little funny, but by the time the air grew warm, I knew it wasn't an accident.

The cup never ran out because God provided.

Not only did He provide this one little $14 need we had, He provided for every need we had. The laundry soap was just a reminder to keep my heart fixed on trusting Him.

Oh, friend, I know it's not easy. The bills pile up and we begin to panic. We begin to plan and calculate how we are going to make this all work out. But we don't have to. God has committed to that. There is no amount of trying on my part that is ever going to make this work. But thankfully, I don't have to.

This simple story is one of many I could share from the years after my husband left. There were big miracles and small laundry soap ones. Miracles that involved financial provision and miracles that provided opportunities, friendship, comfort, guidance, even wisdom.

In all of these years, God has never failed to keep His promise to provide for us. Even in the seemingly small and mundane things, like laundry soap. His provision is beyond what we can imagine. Are you watching and trusting Him for it?

## Getting Deeper with God

Read Psalm 81:10. I imagine you've read many verses before about the provision of God when we are in need. Read this verse with fresh eyes and consider these questions.

*What kinds of things does God promise to provide for me?*

*What does the Bible imply when it says to "open my mouth wide?"*

*One event is mentioned in this verse as evidence of God's provision.*

*What does that make you think about?*

*Are you really trusting Him or do you find yourself trying to "work it out"?*

Be sure to record your thoughts and prayers in your journal. Also take a few moments and list some ways that God has provided for you this week, month, or even year. Remembering these things is a tremendous help when we are waiting for God to provide.

If you need extra encouragement on this topic, get out your Scripture cards that we made on day 7. There is a whole section of verses on trusting God to provide!

# O IS FOR OBEY

I've been praying for you like crazy over the last few days. Let's take a moment to review the steps that we are taking towards victory so far.

*V- Vision check*
*I- Invite Jesus into the mess*
*C- Choose your response*
*T- Trust God to provide*

Today I'm going to have to open a can of worms. I pray that you will read all of my words with grace and love, as I am truly only bringing this up because I want to help you. (Not to start a theological debate that rivals WWII.)

Often Christians get this salvation thing messed up. We read that the Bible says to believe and then we shall be saved. So we pray a little prayer, sit back, and just wait for all the blessings to pile into our laps. We claim that there is absolutely nothing we need to do in order to be saved and thus we can keep right on living this life without much interruption.

The trouble is, that doesn't work very well. If you've been trying that for very long, you might have noticed that those "blessings" aren't turning out quite like you hoped. And you probably find yourself forgetting about that little "prayer" until something awful happens in your life.

I see this happening in churches everywhere today. The trouble is, salvation is about more than a little prayer. It's about more than telling God you believe. That's just the first step. James 2:19 reminds us that even the demons believe in God. He's real. Acknowledging that isn't enough to save us from our sins or restore the relationship that we need and crave with God.

What we need is faith. Not the words, but the THING. You see, faith is really a verb. It's something we do in response to the love that we have for God. It's the only response we could possibly have to true, saving belief in God.

Now don't get all hung up in the age-old debate of faith vs. works or you'll miss the point of this. It's been going on since Jesus' time (hence the necessity of James 2) and we don't want to join in the charade. Instead we want to make a difference in our lives and in the practical sense, it's impossible to make our lives different if we aren't actually DOING something different, right?

But before you go sign up at the local soup kitchen, hear me out on the rest of this. It's not the day-to-day activities that I am targeting here, but rather the obedience of our hearts. Let's dig into the Word and see what I mean.

## Getting Deeper with God

Read Hebrews 11 and underline every time you see the word "faith." If you can make the time, create a chart in your journal listing each person mentioned and the actions that are listed with their name. If you don't have time to do each one, glance through and get an idea of what I'm trying to show you.

Did you notice how active "faith" really is. Faith moves to a far away land (Abraham). Faith builds an ark when it has never rained (Noah). Faith takes a cherished son to the altar for a sacrifice (Abraham). Faith crosses the Red Sea (v.29) and marches around the walls of Jericho (v.30).

Faith obeys God. Did you see it? I'm not telling you to go do something that shows you have faith. I'm simply telling you to OBEY GOD. That's all. Let's finish out today by reading 1 Samuel 15:22 and recording in your journal any thoughts you have about this topic of obedience to God.

Oh friend, I promise I love you. Don't throw any tomatoes at me when you read this chapter. Just trust that I've learned this very same lesson the hard way, and I am praying for you as you ponder it.

By the way, if obedience is something that you or your children really struggle with, consider this Bible study: bit.ly/1QPcNz3 It's written for kids, but I have always found that I learn so much by teaching my kids, don't you? :-)

# R IS FOR REJOICE

*Rejoice in the Lord always and again I say rejoice.* We sang that song over and over again when I was growing up, but I've come to realize that there is one little word that I often ignored.

ALWAYS.

Oh, I have rejoiced in the Lord. I've thanked Him and praised Him for babies, cars, houses, money just when I needed it. You know, all of the blessings that we almost can't help but thank Him for.

But the rest of life has gone by without much rejoicing. I've failed to rejoice in the small stuff. AND I've failed to rejoice in the hard stuff. I've had plenty of bad attitudes and some have really cost me.

If there is anything in my Christian walk that I really wish I had known earlier, it's this. When I finally realized that God was to be thanked regardless of my circumstances and that rejoicing in Him was something I was to do no matter what, everything changed. Let me show you.

## Getting Deeper with God

Read 1 Thessalonians 5:16-18. Write out the three specific things we are instructed to do.

In this passage, Paul is giving the church some very specific instructions. Verses 1-8 of the same chapter tell us WHY we are asked to do these things. What is the reason noted?

I have to admit that I have often gotten hung up on the practical part of how on earth you are supposed to thank God and rejoice over something awful in your life. But that actually isn't what the Bible tells us to do. We are instead called to thank God and to rejoice in Him always BECAUSE of who He is and what He has promised (coming back).

Can you see how totally different that is?

We can be thankful for the hard things because we know that God is who He says He is and because we have nothing but hope in our glorious future. I would really encourage you to get serious about practical ways to do this more in your life.

Although there are many ways to rejoice in the Lord, I think one of the most practical ones is to begin keeping a list of all the things you can thank Him for. Add it to a page in your journal or start a new one that you can keep by your bed. When times are especially hard, going to bed with thankful thoughts makes all the difference.

Need help teaching your kids the art of thankfulness? This post has 6 practical ideas: bit.ly/1TN1zOq. You'll probably find a few things you can put into practice for yourself.

# Y IS FOR YIELD

Remember a few days ago when I described that scene on my living room floor after my husband left?

I've got a confession to make. Although I wouldn't wish that kind of pain on anyone for a single second AND I also wouldn't advocate divorce as a viable option ever, I have to admit that one of the biggest issues I had that day was over the notion of control.

You see, I had worked really hard to get where I was. I made the right grades. Followed the right rules. Married a Christian guy. I had my sights set on the white-picket-fence life and I couldn't bear the thought of giving that up. Divorce was not in my perfect plan.

In fact, the day my husband walked out, I lost complete control over my future as I knew it.

Well, that was what I thought anyway. For way longer than I'd like to admit, I was pretty certain that life as a single mom would no longer contain any white picket fences and that I had just completely blown all chances of being the Proverbs 31 woman I so greatly admired.

Maybe you've felt like this, too. When something tragic happens in our family, we feel the loss of control strangling our very existence. But I've got to tell you a little secret... in case you are still believing the same lies. My friend, YOU ARE NOT IN CONTROL EITHER.

I didn't lose control the day my husband left. I just came to realize the loss that day. The truth is, I never had control to begin with. Oh, let me tell you how hard that lesson is to learn. There is nothing that you or I can do to create the perfect life that we so desperately want. We can spin our wheels, try hard, manipulate, even do great "Christian" things, but we will never be in control.

God always holds the steering wheel. (Proverbs 16:9)

It took me years of tears and heartache to fully come to the realization that this is a good thing. It's not that I wanted everything my way or that I wanted everyone to do what I told them to. It's just that I wanted to be able to do something about my situation. I wanted to be able to do that "right" thing that people suggested and get that desirable result.

But like many before me, the reins were taken completely out of my hands. I find the story of Joseph so inspiring for this reason.

## Getting Deeper with God

If you've never had the opportunity to read the entire story of Joseph from start to finish, consider doing that today. This kind of Bible study is such a wonderful way to see the picture of redemption and the entirety of God's plan for us. (Read Genesis 37, 39, and 40-46.)

In your journal draw a little timeline showing the life of Joseph. As you work through this, note all the times that Joseph was in control of his life.

What did you find? I hope you saw a life full of hard circumstances. Joseph certainly received several difficult sentences that he didn't deserve. It's easy to see that he was not in control of his life at all.

What touches me the most about this story is the ending. Read Genesis 50:15-21. Although Joseph faced many difficult circumstances at the hands of others, he made a CHOICE. (Sound familiar?) He let God take the reins and he purposed himself to respond to his circumstances with faithfulness and obedience. And the result? Well, he was privileged to play the starring role in the saving of the ENTIRE nation of Israel.

That's redemption. And that's the white-picket-fence life that God had for Joseph. Seriously, can it get any better than that?

So now it's your turn to do the yielding. What in your life or your circumstances are you holding on to? What are you afraid of letting God have? Make a list in your journal and pray, asking God to help you trust Him with these things. Then obey. Open your hands and let go of the reins. God's got this under control. He promises.

If you'd like to learn more about Joseph's story and how to trust God in the worst of circumstances, I'd encourage you to check out Fruitful Affliction by my friend Lara Williams. It's a fabulous study.

# WHAT IF IT'S NOT WORKING?

We're more than half way through this book. Can you believe it? For the past week or so we've talked about the specific steps that we need to take in order to rise above our circumstances and become victorious. Let's review them.

V- vision check
I- invite Jesus into the mess
C- choose your response
T- trust God
O- obey
R- rejoice always
Y- yield to God's plan

None of those steps are easy, but all of them are worth the effort. If we can just do these things, we will find great victory no matter what life brings us. But I'm fully aware that you probably still have some questions about how all of this works. Over the next few days we are going to look at some of those big questions that often trip us up.

The first of which is "What if it's not working?"

We try our best to follow the steps and focus on God, but sometimes we feel like it's not working. Our heart doesn't have the peace we desire and we feel once again consumed by all that we are working hard against.

I want to teach you one secret that has been a game-changer

for me. It's simple: speak truth out loud. Might sound odd, but I promise it works. If you feel afraid, speak out loud and tell yourself you are not afraid because God is your refuge and strength. If your hands are shaking and you can't fight back the nerves, speak out loud and tell yourself that God is in control. Ideally, do this with Scripture.

It's a simple secret, but when I started doing it, I was shocked at how much more meaningful it is than saying something in your head or even writing it down. As soon as you speak it, suddenly you feel the depth of its truth.

## Getting Deeper with God

Read Mark 11:20-23. Circle the condition in verse 23 that will move the mountain. You should find two words: says and believes. We see clearly from Jesus' teaching that if we are going to move our mountain (think difficult circumstances), we will need to tell the thing to move and then believe it will. The speaking out loud and believing go hand in hand!

Here are a few more verses to consider. Read them and note in your journal what speaking the Word of God does for you.

Romans 10:10

Revelation 12:11

Hebrews 4:12

Take a few minutes today to write out the truth that you should be speaking over your most consuming circumstance. Then practice saying it out loud as often as possible today.

# BUT THIS IS NOT AT ALL THE WAY I PLANNED IT...

A shame as dirty as the floor washed over me as I pulled the number from the dispenser. Babies wailed and mommas fidgeted. Numbers were called one-by-one. Brokenness filled the room. I couldn't help but wonder about the circumstances that had left each person applying for food stamps that day. Abandoned families. Laid-off employees. Cancer patients. I prayed and reminded myself that God was in control over circumstances. Mine and theirs.

I fought the tears and resolved to maintain control. The moment would finally come when my number was called and she ushered us to her office. Right away, I could see that this social worker was not having a good day. She never looked up. Her tone was condescending and her heart cold. She fired questions at me as if she was hoping to trap me. My situation was bleak and I needed the money, so I endured.

She had no patience, no understanding, and no tact.

On the form, I had checked married, but stated that he left. "That means you are separated, honey," she jeered. I couldn't find the voice to respond, so she continued. "You might as well face it. You are a single mom now." It was the first time I would hear those words and it burned deep. The urge to choke her flooded over me, but I resolved not to come unglued. My heart withered in fear. I had no control over my life and the future was terrifying. I didn't like it, but she was right. I was now a single mom.

Declaring this "status" makes it hard to breathe. The fear of the unknown, the lack of financial resources, the emotional trauma, and the judging eyes all carry great heartache. But for me, my greatest fear is the lack of acceptance. I fear that this will be the one thing that will keep me from being loved.

Single mom.

I picture her living in a trailer, eating cans of beans from the church's food bank, and working while her babes sleep at night. She's tired, mistreated, misunderstood, and often cries herself to sleep at night. Her heart is bitter and lonely and her responsibilities pile much higher than that sink of dirty dishes.

I grew up with this reality and I knew that it was the one thing I never wanted to be. It was the one thing I feared the most. The one thing I worked the hardest to prevent. It wasn't plan A, it was plan Z and I couldn't fathom what God was doing.

But that couldn't be further from the truth. God is always on plan A. He already has it all figured out. He's not surprised, playing catch-up, or wondering what to do. This is something that was impressed on my heart a few years ago by my pastor. God is still on plan A.
If He is fully sovereign, then we can't mess up His plans with our own sinful nature. Let's open the Word and see what I mean.

## Getting Deeper with God

Let's read two verses today: 2 Chronicles 20:6 and Psalm 115:3. What do these two verses tell you about God's sovereignty?

Now let's look at a rather popular verse, Romans 8:28. Write it out in your journal then go back and answer these questions by underlining or marking the answers.

*How many things is God working together?*

*What is God working things together for?*

*What is the condition that I must meet for God to do this for me?*

This may be plan B or Q or even Z for us, but it's not for God. We can trust Him with the absolute BEST plan today. Isn't that great news?

Check-up time: have you memorized Lamentations 3:22-23? How many days this week have you been able to set aside time for God?

# WHAT IS GOD'S PROMISE FOR ME NOW?

One of the hardest parts of losing my husband was letting go of all the dreams that I had spent a lifetime pondering in my heart. I had envisioned this life together, this perfect little family, and now everything was shattered.

I could grasp what the Bible said and truly believed that God was still on plan A even though it sure seemed like plan B to me. (I mean, He hates divorce, right?) What I couldn't fathom was how on earth He was going to fix it. I didn't understand what God's promises for me would be now that there was such brokenness.

Maybe you've wondered the same thing. Sometimes God's answer to such a question is wait, and honestly there are details of that answer that I'm still waiting for 7 years later. But there is actually an answer that we can put our hope in while God works out the details. Let's check it out.

## Getting Deeper with God

Read Isaiah 61:1-4. When I read this passage, I just get so excited I can't stand it. Let's break it down and see what God is saying.

From verse 1, list the particular circumstances that God is sending healing for. Which one is most meaningful to you? Now let's look at verses 2 and 3. Draw or write in your journal the things that God promises and cross out the things that will be replaced.

Isn't this a beautiful picture of what God has promised for you? Yes, I know you want the details of where you will be in 10 years, what your kids will be doing, and what successes you will have. We can't have that. No one can. But we do get to have promises like this one, and friend, isn't this so much better?

You can download a free printable version of Isaiah 61 here: bit.ly/1mmbqwN

# CAN THIS TRIAL REALLY HELP ME?

I remember asking the same question many times to God: *How on earth is this divorce thing going to help me?* Honestly. All I could see were piles of rubble, hurting kids, and a giant scarlet letter D on my chest. I was broken, tossed aside, dirty, used, abused. And probably a few other things I won't mention.

Truthfully, I liked my life a lot better before all of this happened and I wasn't alone.

Just weeks after my husband left, one of my dear friends found out that her son had brain cancer. The roller coaster was brutal. Surgeries. Chemo. Hospitals. Then things seemed ok for a while. Until it came back. More surgeries. Chemo. Hospitals. Finally, there was nothing more they could do. After 4+ years of fighting, their son would meet Jesus.

It's fair to say that both my friend and I would have liked our old lives back. We can't compare the trial that I walked with the one that she did as they both contained their own sets of challenges, ups, downs, heartbreaks, fears, and questions. But they both had many things in common.

Neither of us would sign up for that path again. Neither of us would sign up our worst enemy either. But neither of us would trade the faith that we got in the process. Let's dig into the Word so I can show you what I mean.

## Getting Deeper with God

Read James 1:2-4,12. This is one of those passages in the Bible that we just wish God hadn't included. (Or at least I do anyway. Ha.) Until I got far on the other side of my divorce, I couldn't even fathom what was meant by these words in James.

Now I know. The hard things in life change us one way or another. If you make the choice to grow, remaining strong in the Lord, you will hardly believe your eyes when you get to the other side. People tell me all the time that they can't even believe I'm the same person. I tell you that not to brag on anything I've done. Left to myself, it wouldn't be pretty.

I tell you that because I know first hand what God can do in your life if you let Him. James says that we must remain steadfast if we are to get this blessing. Do you know what that means? It just means to be fixed, constant, non-wavering.

We don't have to be perfect, just faithful. That is the key to our growth. Let's read one more of my favorites today: Romans 4:20-21. Write it in your journal using your name and personal pronouns. It will look something like this:

*No unbelief made Kim waver concerning the promise of God, but she grew strong in her faith as she gave glory to God, fully convinced that God was able to do what he had promised.*

This verse has been on notecards in every single crevice of my house for years now. I may not always like the storm, but I very much like that I can trust God to do what He promised. How about you?

I'd love to connect personally with you. Email me at kim@notconsumed.com and let me know that you are working through this devotional. Let me know how I can specifically pray for you today.

# HELP, I CAN'T HEAR GOD

 When I was about 5 months pregnant with my youngest, I was diagnosed with a placental tear. This is a rather dangerous condition and landed us in the hospital for almost 4 weeks of my pregnancy. By that point, my husband was living with his girlfriend and had to return home temporarily to care for the other kids.

Those days in the hospital were dark. I didn't see my kids much at all. I was left to wonder about all that was going on in my house and family. I had a lot of time to think and a lot of time to worry. I was praying for my marriage to be restored, but God didn't seem to have much to say.

My friends came to the hospital and decorated the walls with Scripture, promises, pictures from my kids, and anything else they could think of to help me stay focused on God's truth. But it was still incredibly hard. In the darkness, I couldn't help but feel like God wasn't working.

I was so lonely and everything was so quiet. I knew God was there and I knew He was working, but I just didn't feel it. Maybe that's where you are, too. If so, I hope today's assignment will bless you richly.

## Getting Deeper with God

Read 1 Kings 19:11-15. In this passage, Elijah is desperately seeking to hear God's voice. Record in your journal the places where he looked for God, but was unable to hear Him. Then note where he actually heard Him.

Depending on the version you are reading, you'll find that God spoke in a still small voice (or a whisper). The more I think of this story, the more I am reminded that if we really want to know God and know His will for our lives, we will need to be still. We can't be frantically going from one thing to another searching. We can't be looking for ways to solve our own problems or "help" God do His part.

We must believe that God will answer. He will fight for us. We need only be still.

Look up Psalm 46:10 and write it in your journal as a reminder to sit still and trust God to do the fixing.

I'm praying for you.

 When I need a reminder, I love to take a little shopping trip to the Christian bookstore. Maybe look for a mug with a good Scripture reminder like this one: bit.ly/23RGwyn

# HOW CAN I GET REAL PEACE IN MY CIRCUMSTANCES?

I think the hardest part about the storm is when it just keeps on raging. Kinda like the thorn in the flesh that Paul mentions in 2 Corinthians 12. There are difficult things in life that keep coming back for more. Circumstances that absolutely won't let up.

Divorce is a good example of this. Many people think that getting closure on the relationship will help things, but it's quite the opposite. If you have kids together, you will have a forced relationship until one of you dies. Maybe not every day contact, but there are new issues that crop up on a regular basis. (This is one big reason that God is so against it, but that's another topic.)

I'm certain that there are other circumstances that bring the same waves of turmoil crashing back in. Just when you think you have the last mess mopped up, the water comes seeping back through the cracks.

**Healing from a difficult trial is not a one time event.** Even if the situation itself doesn't come back up, the issues around it may continue for decades. We need to be aware of this. If we are going to get any sort of victory over these reoccurrences, we will need to be ready to fight.

. . . . . . . . . . . . . . . . . . . . . . . . . . . . . . . . . . . . . . . . . . . . .
## Getting Deeper with God
. . . . . . . . . . . . . . . . . . . . . . . . . . . . . . . . . . . . . . . . . . . . .

Read Philippians 4:6-7. You've probably read this passage before. And if you are like me, you get hung up on the "don't worry" part and never put a whole lot of attention on the rest.

Let's break it down. In verse 6, we are told to do 2 specific things. List them.

Hopefully you saw that we are not to worry (or be anxious) and we are to give God all that concerns us, through prayer and thanksgiving. This part we already know, right? Now read the next part. If we do those two things, what will happen? Underline the word that describes what we get.

Can you imagine having a peace that passes all understanding? Have you ever considered that this peace is given to us by God to guard our hearts? I don't know about you, but that picture just excites me.

To put it another way- NOTHING, absolutely nothing that anyone on this earth does to me, says to me, or takes from me can change the fact that I have access to peace beyond all understanding. My heart is forever guarded... if I am faithful to take all of my anxious thoughts, concerns, worries, and fears straight to God.

There is no promise that the "thorn" or storm will go away. In fact, it's quite possible that the circumstances will just keep right on raging. But we can rest assured that we are sheltered from it through our faithfulness and trust in God.

Finish up today by reading and writing out Isaiah 4:6 and sing "Shelter in the Time of Storm" while rejoicing in these great promises.

I'm praising right along with you,

Sing "Shelter in the Time of Storm"

# REALLY, I CAN HAVE PEACE?

Maybe you're like me and the verse from yesterday is still dancing around in your head. You probably keep thinking about how great it would be if your heart didn't race every time the phone rang. Or how much you'd like to be able to walk back into that hospital without being consumed with despair.

Maybe you'd like to just be able to get up every single day with hope that today won't be as hard as the one before it.
Oh friend, yes, you really can have this peace. And you don't have to wait until heaven to get it. Obviously ultimate peace will be granted there. No more dying, crying, hurting, or sin. But on earth, we are offered the opportunity to have peace even in the midst of those things. All we have to do is continually give God our worry, concern, questions, and fears.

But that's not super easy is it? Let's get some encouragement from the Word today.

## Getting Deeper with God

Read Isaiah 26:1-4. Write out verse 3 completely. This verse is a beautiful promise, but it's easy to miss because of the pronouns. Once you've written it out, look back at the verse and answer these questions:

*What is promised to me?*

*What do I have to do to get that?*

*Who is in charge of keeping this peace for me?*

Did you see it? We do not have to worry about keeping this peace. That's God's job. Our part is to simply stay focused on Him. Now trust me, I know this isn't easy. I also know it's going to take a ton of practice and failed attempts. But it's time to rewrite some of the scripts you've been using in your head.

Every time something threatens your peace, fix your eyes straight on Jesus and don't move them. Tell yourself that He is in control. Recite Isaiah 26:3 or any similar verse that helps you stay focused on the truth of the situation.

When I think of this verse, I can't help but start singing the hymn "Turn your Eyes Upon Jesus." As the song reminds us, when we turn our eyes to Jesus, the things of this earth will grow strangely dim. Such a beautiful promise.

I'm cheering you on!

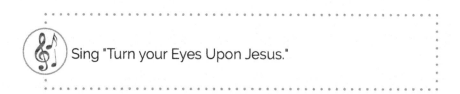

Sing "Turn your Eyes Upon Jesus."

# YOU DON'T UNDERSTAND. MY CIRCUMSTANCES ARE <u>REALLY</u> BAD.

The ceiling in that trauma center is forever etched into my mind. When I woke up, a team of medical professionals was staring at me in some kind of shock. I could feel a breathing tube, monitors, and pain in my chest. But I couldn't feel my legs.

I would later learn that, hours prior, my husband had lost control and ran our van into a concrete pole going 70mph. By God's mercy, I walked away from that accident with major swelling and bruising, and an unharmed baby in my womb.
It wasn't the accident that I'll never forget. It was the ceiling of the hospital that I would see when I closed my eyes at night... for years to come. It was the voice of the chaplain who had been called in to comfort me that would haunt me at night.

The accident itself was rather minor in comparison to the trial that would follow. In the next 9 months, I'd find myself in the hospital more than 9 times with kidney stones, dehydration, and a placental tear. But even that was no big deal compared to the 6 weeks I spent on hospital bed rest. Alone.

What I remember most was the destruction of everything I held sacred. The tears. The ugly words. The rejection. In the same 365 days, I'd get news of the affair, watch my husband move in with his girlfriend, file bankruptcy, and then foreclose on both our houses. I could go on, but I'm hoping you get my point.

I tell you all this because I want you to understand that LOTS of people are walking through really hard circumstances. You're not the only one. You don't have it worse than the other guy. That's a lie the enemy feeds us to just to keep us from believing God.

So I lovingly say to you..."Stop it, ok?" :-) Stop believing this lie. Stop rehearsing this lie. And stop letting the thought even enter your mind. Instead, let's us look at the real truth about your circumstances.

## Getting Deeper with God

Read Psalm 62:1-8 today. Draw or write your response from the reading. Consider illustrating the point that these verses are trying to make.

Now ask yourself these questions:

Does my soul find rest in God alone?

Am I looking to Him alone for salvation?

Am I not allowing circumstances to move me away from God or shake my faith?

Really pray and consider these questions. I want you to be able to answer yes to all of these questions. That is where the true victory is. We have to come to the point where we believe God's promises are true, that He is unchangeable, and thus we are unmovable.

We have to believe that God is able to do exceedingly abundantly and beyond what we could ever think, ask, or imagine. Look up this verse in Ephesians 3:20 and write it out word for word. This is another great one to remember if you are in a trial that will likely be a long time running.

# HOW DO I SLEEP AT NIGHT?

It's 2:19 am. All is still and quiet. But sleep just won't come.

Visions of unpaid bills, never-ending to-do lists, failures, what-ifs, and why-can't-I's dance around as if to taunt the very idea of rest. We think about getting up and accomplishing something, but know that a sleepless night will turn into a nightmare of a day. So we keep trying to drown out the noise in our head and close our eyes a little tighter.

I've found that when things get quiet... the storm gets louder. During the day the kids are needy, school is buzzing, and the house demanding. It's harder to notice the waves swelling. But at night, the noise creeps in.

It's in these moments when we are most weak. We play out scenarios and wonder if we can do better, even tinkering around with feelings of anxiousness and distress. We know better than to let the lies in. But the quiet is so loud all we can do is think.

There is something about the nighttime that has an effect on our ability to fight. Personally, I've spent years struggling with this issue. I'd get one night's rest only to find 3-4 nights where I didn't sleep at all. When the stress of my family situation calmed down, I'd sleep most every night, but only a few hours.

I went years with less than 20 hours of the 56 recommended each week before I realized the effect it was having on me. In fact, it wasn't until I started getting a little more sleep that I finally saw how damaging this had become and how out of control the problem really was.

Friend, if you are struggling to sleep, it's NOT healthy. In fact, it's making everything worse. We need to beat this with a very strong and intentional plan.

# Getting Deeper with God

Let's do another little Bible survey of some of the verses that have helped me the most. Read each one and record in your journal something you learned about sleep, rest, and the night season. You can even write them out if that helps.

Psalm 4:8

Psalm 92:2

Psalm 62:5

Proverbs 3:24-26

Psalm 91:5-7

Psalm 3:5

Some of these verses are the most treasured in my heart because this struggle has been so difficult for me. It's a blessing to think about the sweet comfort God has provided me through this sleep issue.

As a bonus today, I would encourage you to listen to this song: "God Leads Us Along." It's based off Psalm 4:8 and I think it will really bless you.

Sleep sweet, my friend!

 Of course Scripture is the best way to fight anything, but there are a few other practical things you can do to help you sleep. These have worked for me: bit.ly/2oD13HS

# NOW WHAT?

 We've come a long way in the last 29 days. It's my prayer that you've been encouraged beyond what you could ever have imagined and that you now have an arsenal of verses ready to fight your despair, fears, and concerns.

So now what?

You know the truth. You know what to do. But you may find yourself still wondering exactly what your next step should be. Perhaps there are many places in your life that need your attention. I once heard a sermon on this exact topic. The pastor's answer? Just do the next RIGHT thing.

Profound, right? You don't have to fix everything today. Your life is a work in progress. The only way to make changes is to constantly be in the habit of doing the next RIGHT thing. Of course, I can't tell you what that is for you, but I can give you some encouragement for getting it done. Let's dig in.

## Getting Deeper with God

Read Matthew 14:22-33. Can you imagine being Peter? Sometimes I know exactly how he felt. I'm so zealous about something that I fall flat on my face trying to accomplish it! But that's not quite the point I want to make about this story.

You see, Peter did begin sinking in the water. That part is true. But let us not miss that Peter actually DID walk on water. And he met Jesus out there.

Stop a minute and journal an application of those thoughts to your particular circumstances.

The point I want you to see from this story is that you need to get out of the boat. You need to grab hold of the faith that says "walk on water" and then fix your eyes on Jesus. Don't worry about sinking; Jesus will always be there to lift you up. You only need to just start. Do the next RIGHT thing.

 I want you to find someone to help hold you accountable for doing this. A spouse? A friend? A parent? You don't have to give them the dirty details. Just ask them to pray for you as you work on whatever it is that God put in your heart.

# ONE MORE GREAT STEP TO HEALING

I was enjoying a few minutes of much-needed adult time when a lady came flying out of the Chick-fil-A play area. She was screaming for a manager, dragging behind her a toddler who had been scratched badly on his face.

I looked nervously into the play area and confirmed my worst fears. My son was the only other little boy in there. I tried to press down the fear that was swelling up in my heart as I fished him out of the play area.

I made no excuses, but begged for mercy for my little boy who was hurting so greatly. "His daddy left," I whispered "And he isn't taking it well." Thankfully, the victim's mom was gracious and accepted my deep apologies and promises that I was indeed working hard to correct this issue.

I remember that day feeling so helpless. Counseling had been a joke. No one would even see kids as young as he was, but my sweet boy was very much struggling and there was no mistaking the cause.

Hurt people hurt people. It's been said many times before and it remains true. In the situation with my son, this was largely because he didn't know how to express any sort of emotion or talk about what was going on. He was barely 3. But I think there is another reason this happens. Times of suffering are often times of selfishness. We get tunnel vision in our situation and become demanding, self-centered, and crass.

This is something we need to be aware of and working against. We're not the only one in the world having a hard time. It seems like it, but it's not true. We need to stay focused on God's truth, remembering that we have been called to this specific appointment with Him. There's no need to be bitter about it. That can only stand to hurt others.

Paul knew this truth. While the church was suffering great affliction from the Jews, he prayed that they would increase in love.

# Getting Deeper with God

Read 1 Thessalonians 3:12-13. Record any thoughts in your journal.

Now it's time for a self-assessment. Are you hurting people? Are you a single mom guilty of jeering back at married women who complain about their husband working too much? Maybe you are the parent of a child with a chronic illness who sits at the park peering bitterly at the "healthy" children.

This isn't the time to harbor hatred in your heart. The Word says we are to "abound in love," daily increasing our compassion for others. Honestly, this should be easier now. Can't you relate to the pain? Don't you now understand that life isn't as perfect as it seems in those pretty little family Christmas cards we get every year?

Today, come up with at least one person you know who is also struggling. Reach out to them on Facebook or write them a note and mail it. If you can take a meal to someone- do it. Trust me, it's hard to find the energy to give to someone else when you hurt, but it makes all the difference in the healing!

If your kids are struggling with your circumstances, consider the Victorious Family Bundle: bit.ly/20D1jXA. It includes a resource book that I wrote to help parents help their kids when counseling isn't an option. There is also a workbook for kids to go through as you teach them to find God when times are hard.

# TIME TO SURRENDER THE LIST

Remember that list you made on Day 1? I asked you to sit and jot down everything that consumes you. Hopefully you even found things along the way to add to it.

I'd like for you to get it out today and review the items on it. Do you still feel the same way? Hopefully in the past several weeks you've come to a place where none of it seems all that important anymore.

In light of all we've learned... it's time to tear up the list. (Or if you prefer, just mark it out in your journal.)

Using the verses that we've talked about and the promises that God has given you, pray over every single item on that list and give it to God. It's not yours to be concerned with anymore. Then tear it up.

It might sound silly, but sometimes the physical act of removing something can be a very powerful message to our minds.

As you do this, I'd love for you to sing the hymn "I Surrender All." I would encourage you to sing all of the verses and really let the words heal your soul.

*All to Jesus I surrender;*
*All to Him I freely give;*
*I will ever love and trust Him,*
*In His presence daily live.*
*I surrender all,*
*I surrender all;*
*All to Thee, my blessed Savior,*
*I surrender all.*
*I'm praying for you today as you do this.*

Time for a check up. How has God grown you so far in this study? How is your Bible reading and memorization going? What are you growing in?

# IT'S TIME TO LAUGH AT THE FUTURE

In February of 2013, I packed up my 4 kids and moved to a new state for my dream job. That spring I worked like crazy, enjoyed every minute of it, and received nothing but accolades from the boss. But as the summer heat droned on, it became increasingly obvious that my main job wasn't going well. The event type I was hired to run didn't quite hit it off. People had loved the traditional homeschool convention idea, but this new short and sweet method was not such a hit.

By the time my boss called me with the news that he could no longer afford my salary, I really wasn't all that surprised. He generously gave me 30 days notice, which included pay.

But I was in a bit of a pickle. My rent was far more than I could pay and the income from other sources was pathetic and inconsistent. I had 4 kids who always seemed to expect meals and from what anyone on the outside could tell, the waves were once again crashing havoc on my already tired heart.

I remember sitting on my bed that night and laughing. Yes, I said laughing. But not the laughing of unbelief like Sarah did in Genesis 18. My laughter was more like the Proverbs 31 woman (see verse 25).

There wasn't an ounce of fear, distress, or even disappointment in my heart that night. I laughed because I was excited, or as the KJV version puts it, I "rejoiced in time to come." You see, I

knew that God was closing this door which meant that there would be another door in the future.
And truthfully, I couldn't wait to find it.

I knew that the next day I would have to file unemployment and even ask for food stamps. Two things which had brought such shame over me in prior years. But my years of suffering and heartache from the betrayal and abandonment had taught me a valuable lesson and I didn't miss it this time. I knew God could be trusted for good (Romans 8:28). And I knew He could be trusted for that which was beyond my imagination (Ephesians 3:20).

So my question to you is this... can you laugh at the future? Can you rejoice knowing that God has nothing but your good in mind?

## Getting Deeper with God

Read Proverbs 31:25 and replace the pronouns with your name. Declare this verse over yourself and then write a list of the things you look forward to seeing God do in your life.

# FAKE IT UNTIL YOU MAKE IT

You've heard it said: fake it 'til you make it.

In some ways this is wise advice. It's wise because our feelings aren't reliable. They can't be trusted with the truth (Jer. 17:9). We might not feel like trusting God, getting out of bed, or putting on a smile for the kids. This is where we "fake it until we make it."

Most of us have done this before when it comes to getting out of bed. You put one leg over the edge of the bed and push the rest of your body out. No matter how tired you feel, most of the time you can go about the day within a few minutes of "faking it" or getting out of bed.

I think this "fake it until you make it" thing is true with trusting God, too. Sometimes we feel weak and we can't see a good outcome to the situation. We have to walk forward trusting God even if we don't feel like we are 100% in that trusting place.

But today I'd like to talk about this concept in regard to your kids, if you have any. (If not, for rest of this devotional think about your spouse, family, or coworkers when I say the word kids.)

Has it occurred to you that they are watching you?

They see every tear (even the ones you don't know they see). They hear the fear in your voice. They know the pain in your heart. EVEN if you are trying to hide it. I have to admit that this is one thing that really upsets me when I see parents doing it.

We're given children for just a season, so that we might teach them to love God with a faith that can weather any storm life throws at them. But then we hide the tears and don't share real life with them. How does that even make sense?

Of course, I'm not suggesting that you need to share every dirty detail of a situation with your 4-year-old. That's silly. But when the tears fall, why not say something simple like, "Baby, mama is sad right now but I know that God is helping me." Don't over think it. And don't worry about messing up. God's got your back.

After 7 years of storm, I'd say that I'm on the other side of the worst of it. When I look around at the other children from our church, it's painfully obvious that mine are different. In some ways, I hurt for them. But in some ways it's also beautiful.

You see, my kids know faith. They know what it's like to pray for enough food to eat for dinner that night because I encouraged them to. I wanted them to see God provide because I knew He would.

They've watched me cry when the pain was unbearable and they've heard me praise the Lord in the same breath. That's what I mean by "fake it until you make it." There were times when I really didn't want to give thanks in all circumstances. There were times when I wanted to throw myself on the floor and throw an all out 2-year-old tantrum. I just knew it would feel good. BUT- I knew they were watching and I wanted them to know a better way.

One day they will walk through a storm (probably many) and I want them to learn from me so they won't drown. Telling myself now that I hope they don't experience trials is plain foolish. The Bible promises they will, so I need to prepare them.

# Getting Deeper with God

Start today by reading Deuteronomy 6:4-7. This is our ultimate calling as parents. Write down any thoughts you have.

I'd also really like for you to think practically and intentionally about pouring into your kids spiritually. Many lessons will be done as life happens and the moment presents itself, but we also need to be prepared. Write down your plans and commit to them.

Here are a few tools I have written that might help:

Developing a Quiet Time bit.ly/1Q2XgZe_is a bible study for kids 8 and up, helping them develop the why and how behind spending time daily with God.

A Content Heart bit.ly/1nXF914 is a study helping kids find contentment within their circumstances. There are two levels spanning ages 4- adult.

Foundations of Faith bit.ly/1nXFhgQ is a family study designed to help you establish core beliefs as a family. The study has suggested resources, questions to ponder, and space to record your statement of faith regarding each of the key issues we face today.

Whatever you do, please don't let this slip because you are busy. Your kids need you to be intentional about showing them who God is so they can know how to rely on Him when they need Him most.

# THE STEP YOU CAN'T AFFORD TO MISS

The sky was dark and the alarm clock taunted my sleeping body. It was just after 5am and we were on vacation. The thought was fairly understandable: *Why on earth did I set that alarm?*

Oh yes, I remember.

I scrambled to my feet and announced that it was time for everyone to jump in the car. All 4 children were startled but quickly full of excitement. We piled in the car and drove the 1 mile to the beach.

The morning was a little chilly for Florida, but it didn't seem to bother anyone. We made ourselves a spot on the beach under a blanket and cuddled close. At first we sat for what seemed liked hours just talking and praying and remembering all the wonderful things that God had given us on this special trip.

And then it finally happened. A tiny speck of light appeared out of the vast darkness and the squeals could not be contained. "There it is! The sun is coming up!" We watched on the tips of our chairs (ok the tip of the sand) as each beam peeked into the sky.

I'll be honest. It was probably one of the most beautiful things I have ever seen. I don't know if it was the reminder of God's goodness or the squeezing of those excited little hands, but my heart was so full that I thought it might burst.

You see, our family worked very hard at building the unity that we needed to not just survive the storms we were facing, but to rise victorious in the circumstances. For years we had been hanging on by a thread, or so it seemed.

But that morning on the beach, God reminded me of all His glorious works and I saw all of that and more. It didn't come in a fancy package or an amazing activity. (In fact, that trip to the beach was completely free.)

The beauty came from a simple sacrifice of my agenda to spend time pouring into their lives.

The placement of this chapter in the book is very intentional. Getting yourself right with God is an absolute priority. It's the only time I agree with the statement of "put yourself first." You simply can't help anyone else if you are living in darkness.

But now that you KNOW that you aren't living like that anymore and you are claiming God's promises over each and every day (even if they are still hard), it's time to remember what's important in our lives.

Family.

What we all really want is to have that family we have always wanted. We want to feel and experience the joy of family. This starts in our own hearts and in the expectations we bring to the party, of course. But there are some intentional ways we can build the family unity that will hold us together through the storms of life.

Are you game? I hope so, because I have created a free ebook for you that I know you won't want to miss. It's 10 core ways to build family unity, with over 100 practical ideas. Each way is a principle that you can apply to your life today. These ideas will serve as a guide and resource to help you build a family that will stand strong together no matter what life brings.

You can refer to the book or print the pages to keep in your homemaking binder or even hang on the fridge. (Most ideas do contain clickable links though, so keep that in mind!)

I'm so thankful for you and I pray that this resource is such a blessing to your family!

Download your copy of the free ebook here: bit.ly/1PIUZGJ

## Day 36

# BEFORE WE SAY GOODBYE

 We have come so far in this devotional. I'm so proud of you for enduring. Just sticking with the reading of each day was a huge commitment and I hope it blessed your walk with the Lord. Before I send you off, though, there are a few things I want to make sure we accomplish.

We can easily see our need for trusting God when our whole life comes crashing down, but we can be guilty of missing that need when it's just a pile of dishes in the sink. There are practical life things that might help you survive and thrive in the midst of a storm. I want to equip you with a few tips to make sure the little things are not going to take you down.

- Taking control of your schedule/routine bit.ly/1T8a5rE
- Get your kitchen and meal planning in order bit.ly/1T8ao5T
- Chores that will actually get the work done bit.ly/1QQ6KdE

Remember, we aren't going to be looking for perfection here. Instead we want to learn to do all of this through obedience and trust in the Lord. I pray these posts bless you.

## Getting Deeper with God

Today we need to sit down and reflect on what God has done for us. Let's read Joshua 4. I know it's a long chapter, but I promise it will be worth it. After 40 years of wandering in the wilderness, the Israelites are finally making their way into the promised land. They have just crossed the Jordan River where God again parted the waters for them to cross. Go ahead--read and see what happens...

I actually think that this might be one of my favorite stories in the Bible. Here they are, after experiencing such an amazing miracle yet again, anxious to be where God promised they would be, and He takes the time to graciously remind them to never forget what He has done for them.

Ya know, in my life I've noticed that I'm ever so guilty of forgetting these things, too. As soon as the waves come crashing back in, it's almost as if I've forgotten that God has indeed done something beautiful in my life. So today I have this task for you. Write out a prayer of thanksgiving, recording the things God has done for you. You might even consider keeping an ongoing list of miracles in your journal.

This might be from our study time together. It could be something from years ago. You don't have to see the light at the end of your present "tunnel" in order to remember how God has brought you out of the tunnels in your past.

I'm praying for you, my friend. This time together has been so sweet. I have seen God working in lives each day. Keep fighting the fight of faith. Don't give up. God's loving kindness will carry you, comfort you, and remake you into exactly what He wants you to be!

If you have a testimony to share or feedback to offer about this study, please email me at kim@notconsumed.com. I very much want to know, and love praying and praising the Lord with you!